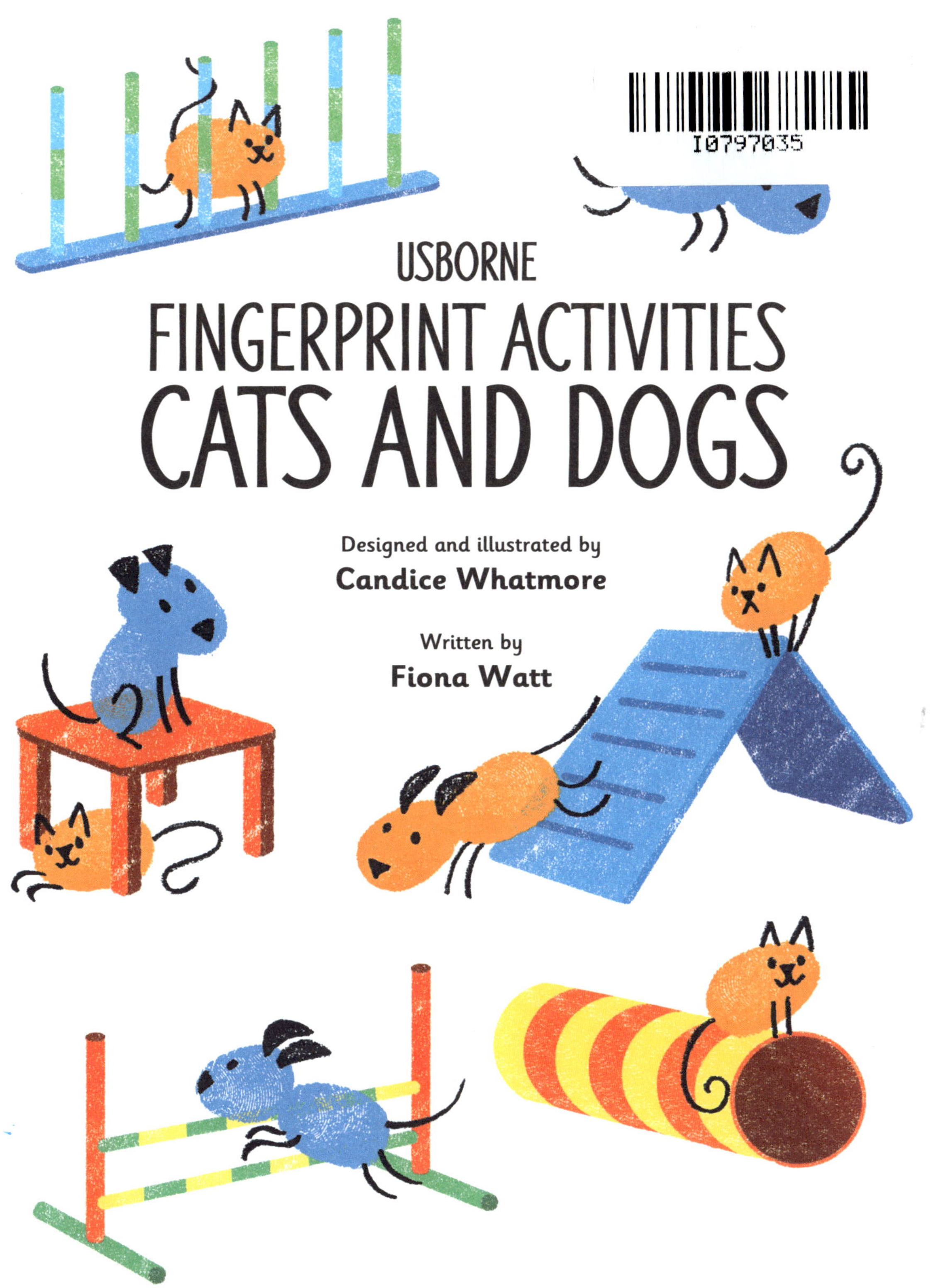

USBORNE

FINGERPRINT ACTIVITIES CATS AND DOGS

Designed and illustrated by

Candice Whatmore

Written by

Fiona Watt

FINGERPRINTING TIPS

Press your finger onto one of the ink pads a few times to make sure you have a nice inky finger before printing it in the book.

Clean your inky fingers on a paper towel when you want to use a different ink. When you've finished printing, wash your hands with soap and water to get rid of any ink stains.

Try not to get the inks on your clothes or work surface as they may stain them. Don't lick your fingers - the inks won't taste very nice.

Use different fingers to make different sizes of prints. You can use the very tip of your finger to make a round print.

Finger tip

First finger

Thumb

Wait for your fingerprints to dry completely before drawing on them with felt-tip pens or crayons.

Print markings on the cat's head, body and tail.

Add dogs for the busy groomers to brush and dry.

1.

2.

3.

4.

5.

POOCHY
DOG
shampoo

SWEET♥PAWS
spritz spray

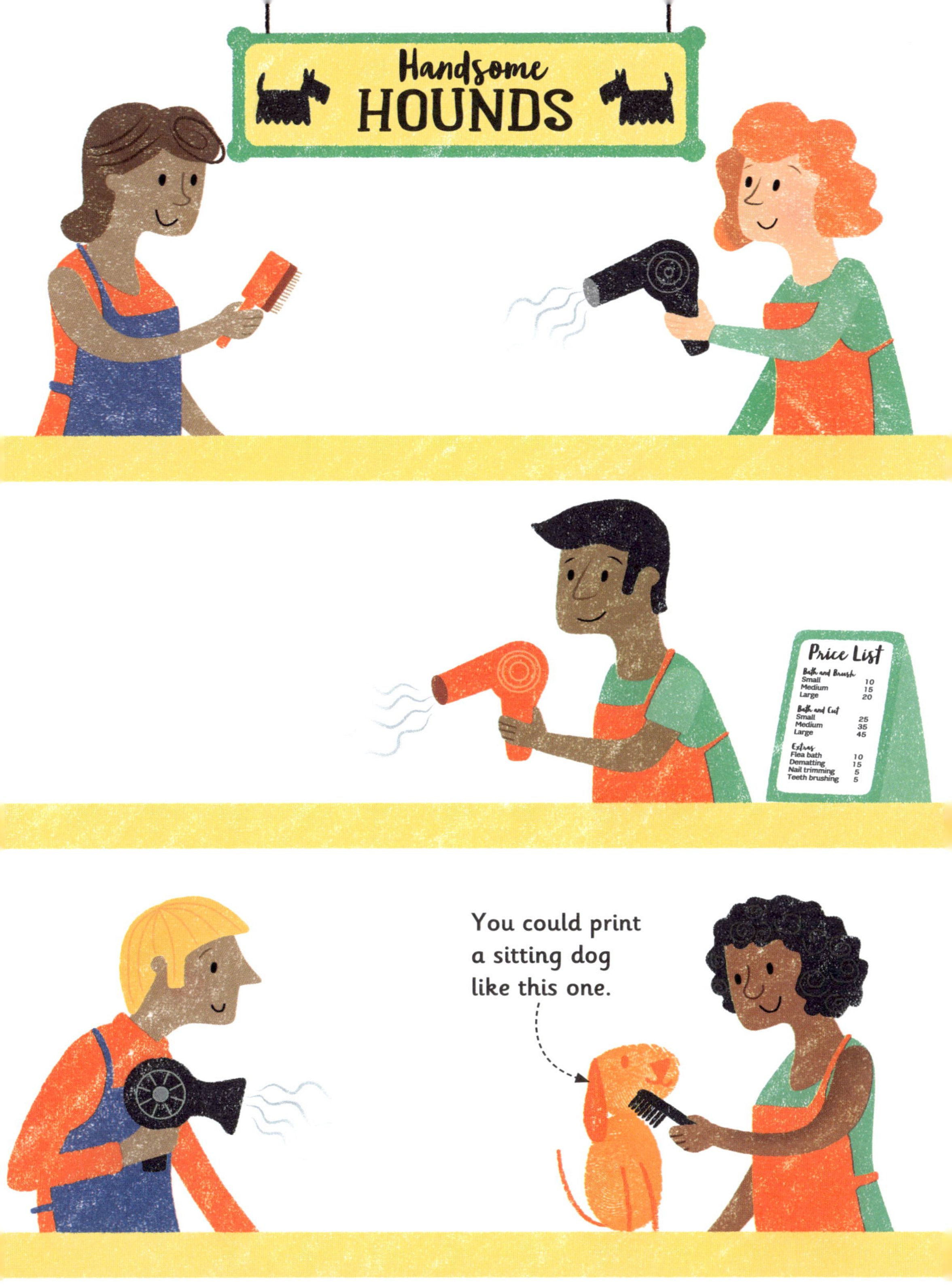
Handsome HOUNDS
Price List
Bath and Brush
Small 10
Medium 15
Large 20
Bath and Cut
Small 25
Medium 35
Large 45
Extras
Flea bath 10
Dematting 15
Nail trimming 5
Teeth brushing 5
You could print a sitting dog like this one.

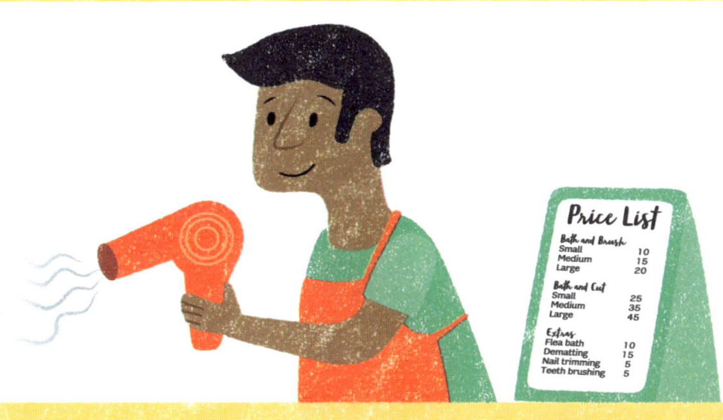

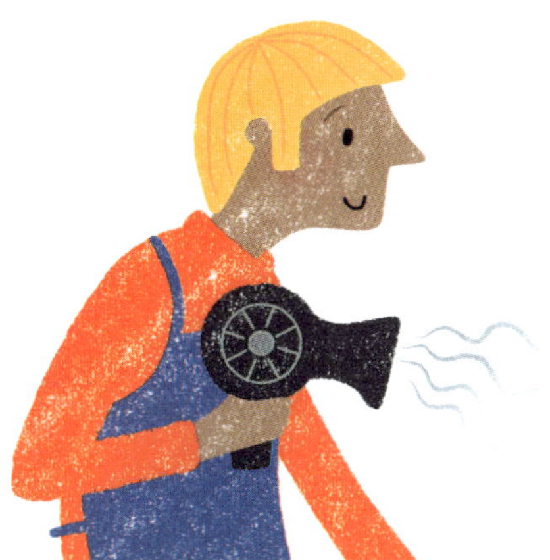

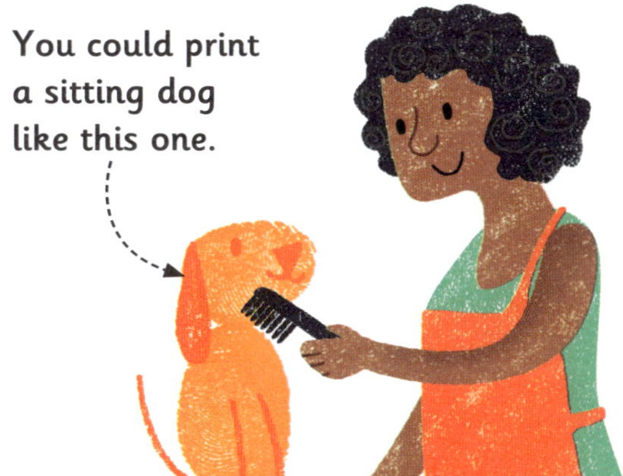

Add more alley cats prowling around...

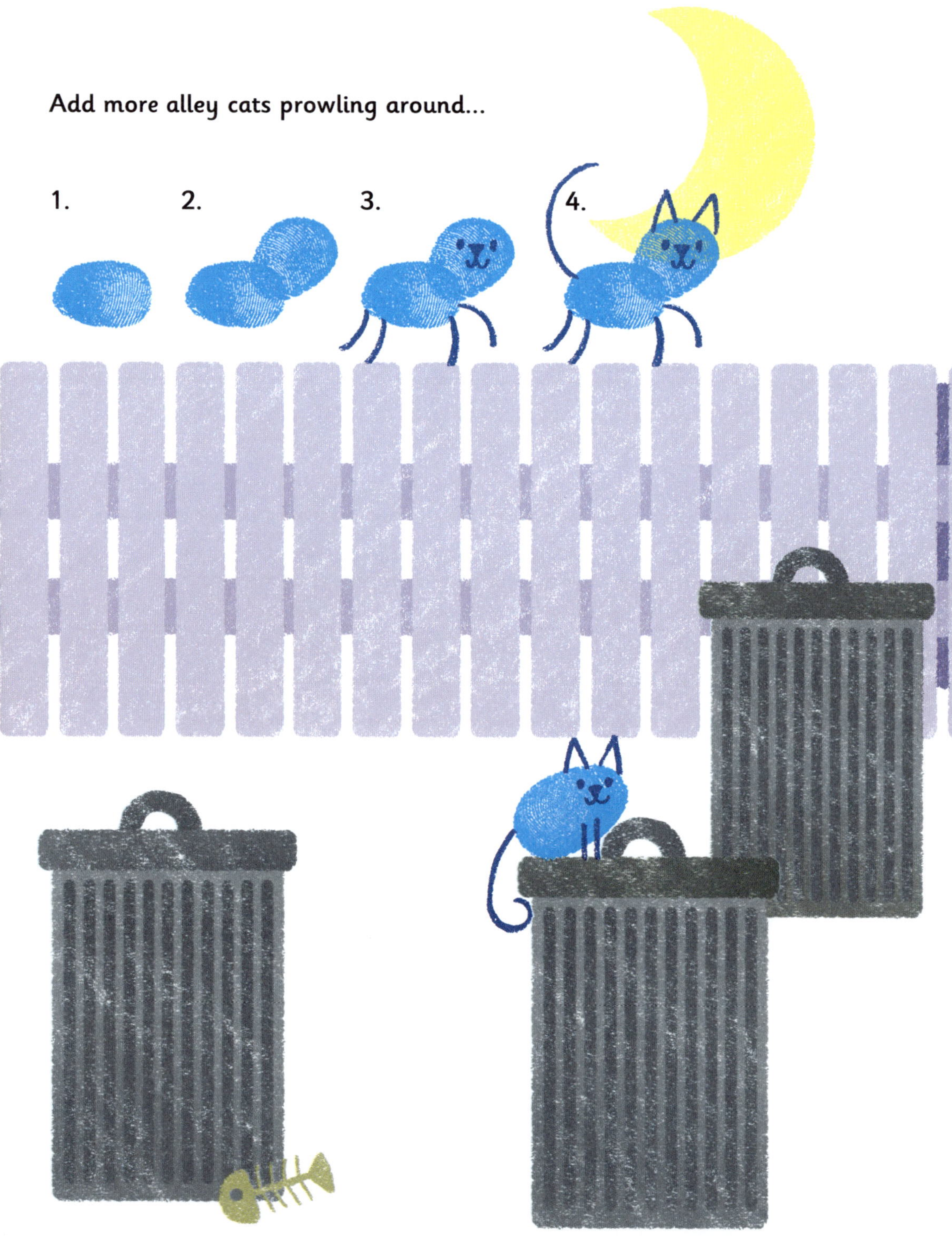

...or sitting down.
1.
2.
3.
4.

DOG
SHAMPOO
Paws
SHAMPOO AND SHINE

Fingerprint lots of bubbles around these dogs having a bath.

Print more cats playing with balls.

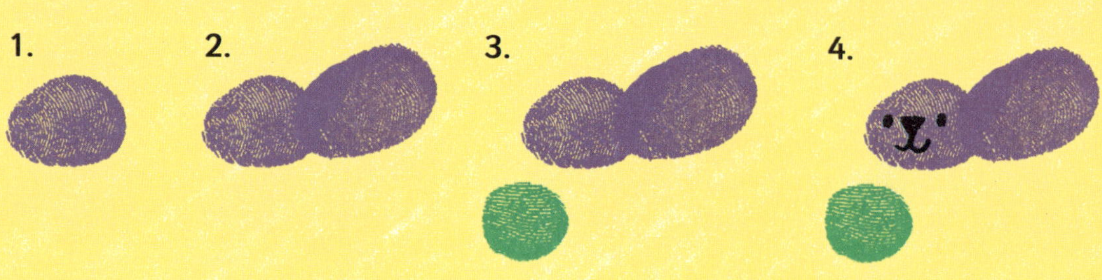

5.
6.
7.

Fingerprint pink poodles walking along this street in Paris.

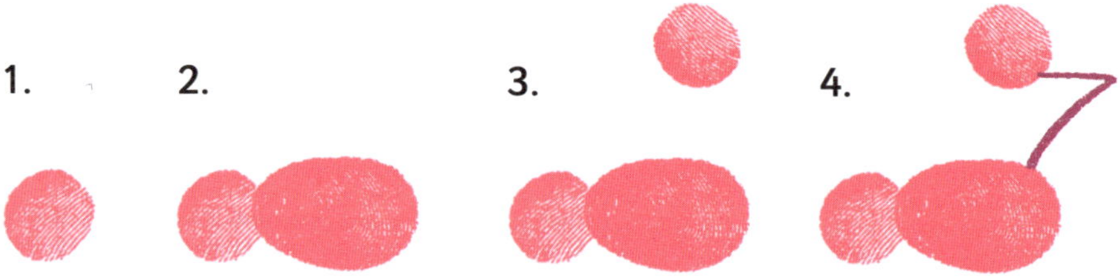

1.

2.

3.

4.

5.

6.

7.

Fingerprint cats sleeping on the sofas and chairs.

Dixie

Print spots all over these Dalmatians.

The muddy dog and cat have walked over a clean floor! Add more of their paw prints.

Use the tip of your little finger for the cat prints.

1.
2.
Use your
thumb for
the dog prints.

Print naughty cats trying to grab the goldfish.

Some cats just like
to watch the fish.

Oh dear!
This one
fell in.

1.
2.
3.
4.

Fingerprint dogs out for a walk with their owners.

Fingerprint more mice running away from the cats.
1.
2.
3.
4.

Print lots of dachshunds playing in the park.

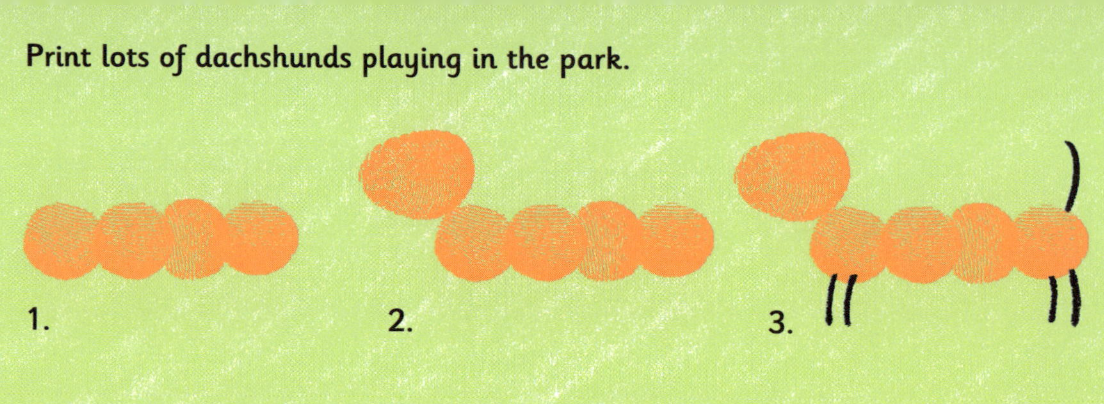

4.
5.

You could try changing the positions of the head and legs.

Use your little finger to print eyes on these kittens.

Use your thumb to print a bulldog's head and body.

For a running bulldog, draw the legs like this.

This bulldog is
lying down.

Add a nose to each of
these dog portraits.

Print food in each of the hungry cats' bowls.

Print little pomeranians. They are so small they could fit into a bag.

Print lots of cats playing, sleeping, sitting and scratching on this cat tower.

Try different poses
by changing the
legs and tail.

Add lots of tiny Chihuahuas playing together.

Print eye spots on these bull terriers.

Add more cats staying at the animal shelter. Show them standing...

1. 2. 3.

4. 5.

sitting...

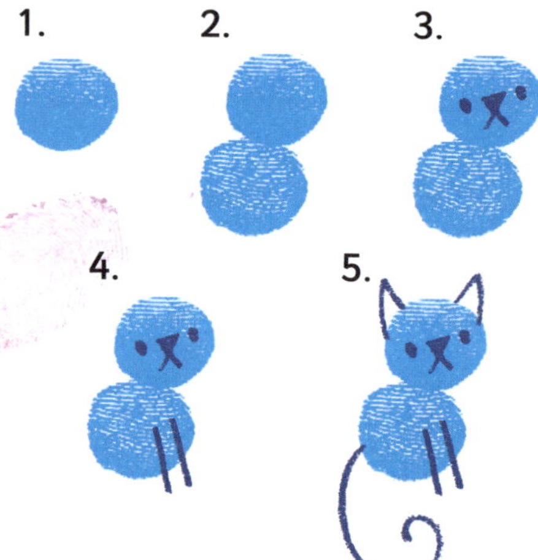

or sleeping.

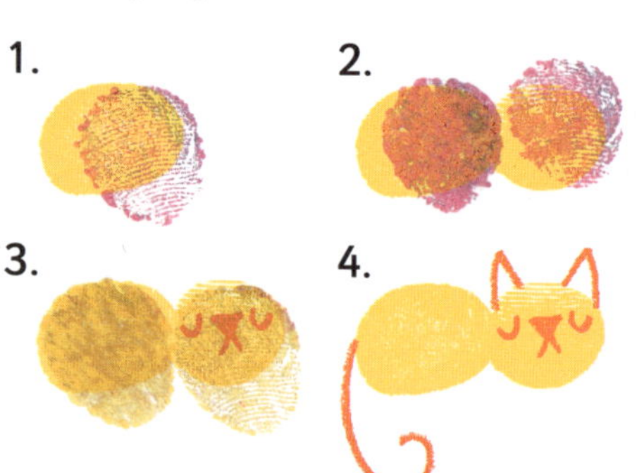

12 Rani and Raj

Give the cats names.

22

13

14

23

24

Print more sniffer dogs checking the bags at the airport.

3
BAGGAGE
FLIGHT DD4762

Fingerprint more fluffy fur on the tail, feet, chest and head of these poodles.

Add birds perched on the bird table and washing line.
1.
2.
3.
Fingerprint lots of birds on the patio, too.

1.
2.
3.
4.
Add cats watching the birds
through the windows.

CUTEST DOG

Add 1st, 2nd and 3rd ribbons on the dogs in the order you think they deserve.

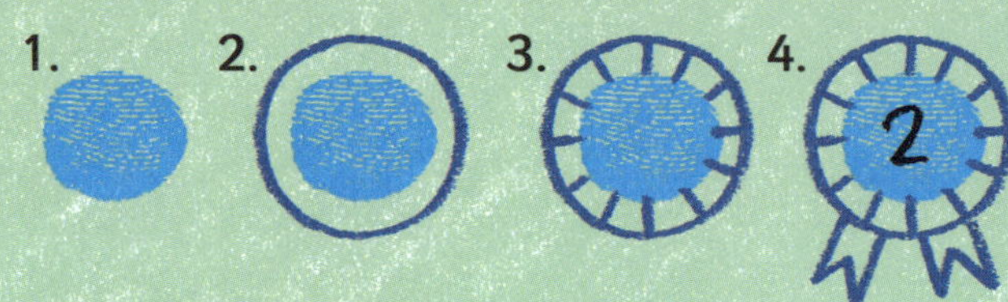

MOST HANDSOME DOG

BEST COSTUME
BEST IN SHOW

Print lots of cats hiding in the trees.

1. 2. 3.

You could add leaves to hide them too.

Add dogs running around the agility course.
Copy the positions below.

Running

Jumping

Sitting

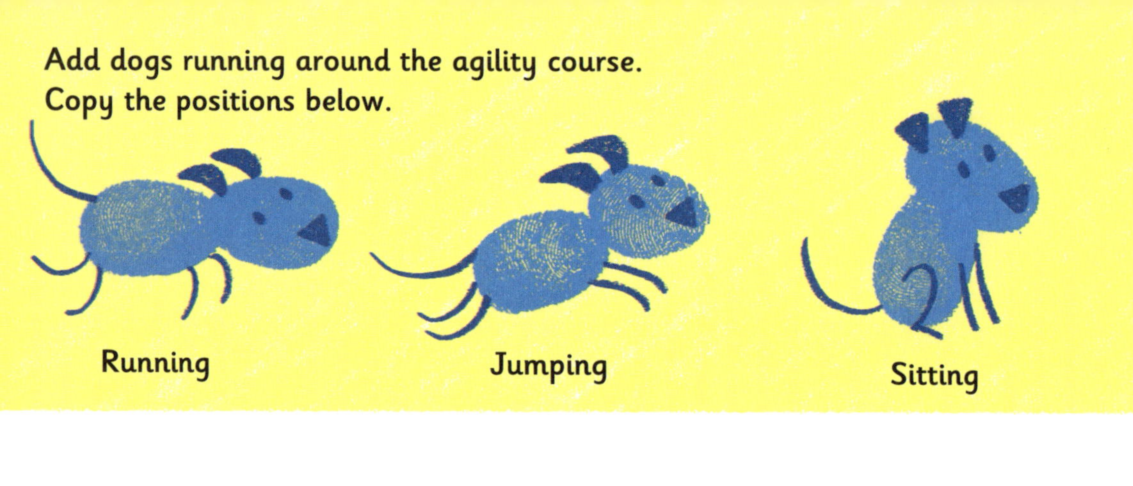

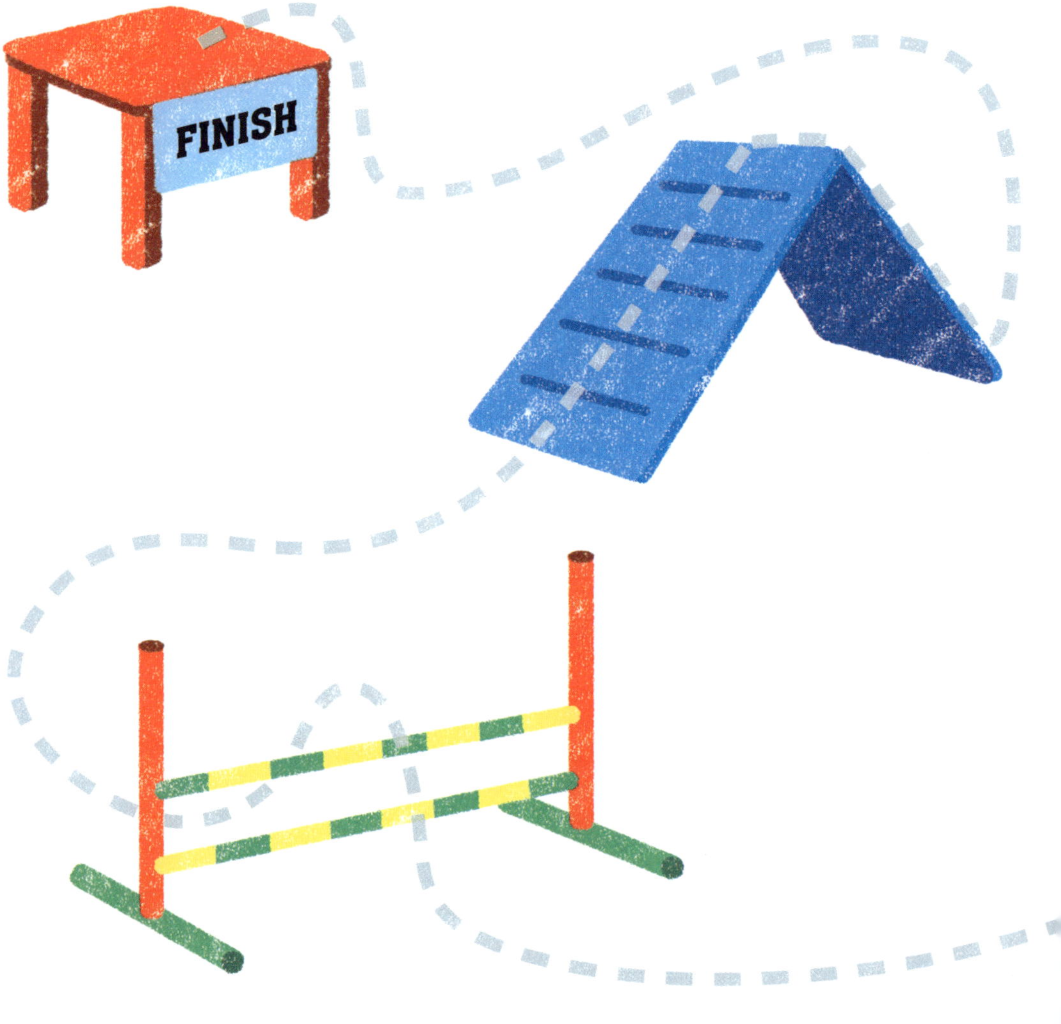

START

Print a 'beard' on these schnauzers, then draw a nose and mouth.

1.

2.

Print some friendly cats rubbing themselves on their owners' legs.

Some people
might have
two cats!

Add puppies to the dog baskets.

Print some kittens on this page.

Decorate the greyhounds' coats with spots.

First published in 2020 by Usborne Publishing Limited, 83-85 Saffron Hill, London EC1N 8RT, United Kingdom.
usborne.com
First published in America 2020. This edition published 2025. UE.